Outfoxing Hyenas

Alan Price

Indigo Dreams Publishing

First Edition: Outfoxing Hyenas
First published in Great Britain in 2012 by:
Indigo Dreams Publishing
132 Hinckley Road
Stoney Stanton
Leicestershire
LE9 4LN

www.indigodreams.co.uk

ISBN 978-1-909357-00-6

British Library Cataloguing in Publication Data. A CIP record for this book can be obtained from the British Library.

Designed and typeset in Palatino Linotype by Indigo Dreams.

Cover design by Ronnie Goodyer at Indigo Dreams.

Printed and bound in Great Britain by Imprint Academic, Exeter on paper and board sourced from sustainable forests.

to Marcus Revell

Acknowledgements

Some of these poems have been published in the following magazines: *Envoi, Orbis, Obsessed With Pipework, Poetry Monthly, Essence, The Interpreter's House* and *The Delinquent*. Some have also featured in the following anthologies: Seeking Refuge, Postcards from Leather Lane, A Shadow on the Wall, Genius Floored and Alphabet Days.

The help and support of Alan Brownjohn and Louise Warren has been greatly appreciated.

CONTENTS

Travelling Lighter

Assorted Histories

Destinies

Outfoxing Hyenas

Travelling Lighter

How Many Stories of Rivers

Once there was a grandfather
who died at the docks riveting
cabin holes into a ferry boat,
till an idiot chain knocked him
acrobatically into the Mersey.

Once there was a girl, my mother,
who juggled grief with two sisters
by watching very hard a silent film
set at night on the river Thames.

Pregnant, with me, she dreamt of both
rivers overlapping all face of family.
I left her face for a Sussex coast.
Home fracturing all my voyages.

Drinking beer by the Ganges or Danube.
More stories carried on burning.
Hot rivets, with voices, that I never allowed
to be cooled in the waters.

How many stories of rivers can we allow.
Do they take us to or away from ourselves.
Have we shed a dependable river god
and dislocated Homer's journey?

Pretence of a Waitress

Thick black hair. Sheen pitched
to raven feather caught
in early morning.

Sleep hiding in a young woman's
eye. Rubbing her tiredness
with sunburnt knuckle of hand.

Pensive. Stretching, yawning
at the long hot work day ahead.
Grey green her cautious eyes.

Jeans for thin, kept busy, legs.
Half unbuttoned white shirt
shielding her small breasts.

Precise, yet luminous body.
A woman clearing the tables
by the harbour at Corfu.

Distracted by children, she spilt
my breakfast coffee. Bread
and omelette fell into the sand.

Ferry boat filling up. Sipping
a re-fill of bitter coffee.
I left her small change.

Hit the Land of Combray

Sweaty and ageing ten rupee note
torn by a grasping railway guard.
Reluctant bribe. Panicky darkness.
Passengers beaten by a ruthless stick.
The light flickers. The menagerie settles.
Crushed against my backpack Proust.
Three volumes, save me, of broken spines.

A singing beggar, with impresario child,
accompanies the smell of flesh and hot food,
power cuts, strong sugared chai
and gritty demands to practice English.

Noisy claw of a crowded carriage
attacking the long elegant weave
of a Proustian sentence.
Ear plugs, as precious as diamonds,
now lost in the dirt.
Eighteen hours from Trivandrum to Calcutta.
What can I do with my rail time Marcel,
where is your languor – your scenes of Combray?

Swann, in love, finally implodes his jealousy.
We are pushed to the edge, forced to shout.
Keep still! Keep quiet! Move on train!
Please let us just hit the land of Combray,
and get off at the Budding Grove.

Hidden Book

Broken spine forced against cufflinks.
Camouflaged by crisp folded shirts.
Hidden away. Suppressed by wardrobe.
Boy exposing book to the light.
The Camp on Blood Island extricated.
Revealing its execution book cover.
British P.O.W. kneeling, head bowed.
Raised sword of Japanese soldier.
Half naked. Sweating. Bestially intent.
'Shame' of the prisoner pulsating through
the enemy, waiting for a grisly music cue.
Imperial musician - now perform.
Decapitate. Swish of the blade.
Cymbals clashing. No head rolled.
Footsteps of liberation, behind the door.
Older brother rescuing the invaded camp.
Blood throbbing hand. Child's wrist burning.
Book falling. Captured. Confined to its clothes.

Chronos

Barefoot boy ascending a steep staircase.
Falling on a Timex watch.
Crushing Alpha and Omega.
A watch finger pricking his heel.
Speckled blood on carpet and stair rod.
Mother consoling her son. Unmeasured time.
Father revealed as the un-protector.
Horology his compulsive
and easier love child.

An irascible man plucked out time's arrow.
Three days he hunted for the lost part.
Filthy room, inner sanctum, top of the stairs.
Dirty table, dirty rags for oil stained objects.
Clocks. Watches. Time uncovered, anatomically exposed.
Naked hair and main spring shielded by a face.
Each dial containing a hurrying short story.
Nine fifteen. Four thirty. Twenty four after death.

Mother kissing a removable plaster.
Child's skin throbbing with expectation.
They look up at a vast closed door,
slowly approach and knock hard.
Chronos, once a white horse on the sun
god's chariot of time, has been mutated
to an ordinary guy who removes his eye glass,
turns and listens.

What shall we do about the flesh, Walter?

Nudes of Ingres conglomerating in Sickert's head.
Fleshy ladies, choc a bloc, in a Turkish bath.
Clear off you women of Salon de Paris!
Give me a plain earthy nude pinned to a mattress.
Ripper encrusted – dark browns and greens for good old Jack!

Woman on bed. Man over bed. Paint on the bed.
Woman on bed. Man seated on bed. Paint off the bed.
Pay the rent, end the affair, start a new conversation.
You're doing my head in, Walter.
Stop changing your story.
Come in for questioning!

Arm folded standing customer. Short changed by copulation.
She, apprehensive or calm, trying to turn away.
Shielding herself from morose story tellers.
Her splayed fat, sweating with genitals, twitching
for a moment, whilst she empties her eyes
of all who paid for the painted silence.

Temptation

Naked sleeping tight on a brute landslip.
Fine brown hair braided back for ceremony.

Curvaceously tired of sex, or sex waiting.
Fully whitened arm dangling over a hole.

Will Antiope roll in…fall deadly asleep?
Trees, exposed to the root, leer at the chasm.

Zeus has pulled back her vegetal covering.
Jumped up muscular satyr, swarthy of earth.

What he does next is no one's business.
Unless she resists, gives him the Apollo eye.

Moon Violence, A Dream in Three Parts

(1)

La Luna perspiring, beckoning.
Entering the lift shaft, ascending.

Moon full. Horrifically bright.
Sprung from tarot card to sky.

Pressing soft each crack and crevice.
Desiring a watcher at three am.

My fate caught on the twentieth floor.
Light coating my skin and schema.

(2)

Child's silver house bolted tight.
Can a father actually howl at the moon?

Doctor, with husky voice, prescribing.
Warning a mother. Sub-normal man.

Leave and you'll get next to nothing.
Stay. Just don't ask for the moon.

A mother's fury. Pitched to illuminate.
Striking, with poker, her husband's knee.

Cowering white on his moaning chair.
See, her lunacy approaching.

Running to the shade of outside toilet.
Peeing afraid. The white light comes.

(3)

I waver in my sleep, silver collecting.
Stumbling through an empty corridor.

Nobody over bed. Nobody in lift.
No dream. Moon simply trying to hang.

Swimming Lesson

Adriatic declines
its blue finesse
to the replete white
of laden rocks
that leak hot
black smiles,
each broken cavity
weakly sipping
the wet and the dry.

He balanced his nerves
on the lido stone.
Desiring movement
through still sand.

To the left, scorched couples.
To the right, a lizard hunting shade.
Behind, jazz cut on a clatter of plates.
In front, a mother ducking her son.

He couldn't swim then.
Forgot where he was.
What humans do.
What they contain.
The coolness of why.

Cleaning is Life

Flat capsizing with videos, music and books.
Dust scattered on the lost and untidy.
Perilous corridor. Sharp intake of breath.
It is like a dream…a film…have I been here before?
Machiko fingering the mess as if first blossom.
Surveying all objects, exempting their soul.
A Japanese 'actress' on surface location.
Things cannot wait. Cleaning is life!

Rock garden at Riyonji temple, Kyoto.
Oven door in a Camden high rise, London.
Zen arrangement. Fifteen rocks on white gravel.
As contemplative as a dirty second-hand cooker.
Machiko kneeling, cloth in hand.
Bent for purpose. Quiet prayer of cleaning.
He asked why this? Entreated her to stop.
Things cannot wait. Cleaning is life!

Diminutive breasts, strong bolts of red nipple.
The hoop of my arm encircled her waist.
Disturbed blouse of sweat. Brushed hard the kitchen.
Fingertips gripping the stain. Machiko feigning collapse.
He pulled her up. Laughing she covered her chest.
Gas rings, grill and enamel hating distraction.
Let us cook food now…set table…open the wine.
Things cannot wait. Cleaning is life.
My boss said so. He must be right!

Lowering the Transmission

She went to a hospital that still treated the poor.
She recited, to herself, the surgeon's language.
She knew her disease like a memorised poem.
She took a bag of books with William Blake on top.
She kept knocking the books off the table.
She let Songs of Innocence & Experience get dented.
She finally opened and read its profundities.
She became, for an hour, Blake's pellucid words.
She saw her blighted lung as if in a vision.
She kicked it through the chartered streets.
She let it bleed against a wall.
She hurled it hard into the Thames.
She felt sick from over-eating on a prophet.
She drank water to lower the transmission.
She hid her fear behind thick newspapers.
She found True Confessions stuck inside.
She sucked on silly romances to blunt the edge.
She survived the operation and went home to her son.
She found him piping & dancing in a Blakean design.
She kissed the boy and walked to her garden.
She saw trodden flowers, at dusk, on the injured earth.
She heard someone clear their throat in the darkness.
She turned and saw the watcher of the night.
She sensed he had lost his place in the book.
She didn't escape nor ask to be read to.
She sang of what was left, and why it was real.

Would Be Writer

Hungry she came to the writers group.
She'd cut her finger and was pretty drunk.
After sizing up the writers she spoke to me,
half revealing a bloody exercise book.
I stared too hard at pages of scribble.
She worked late shifts at a big casino
where men gorged long on cards & the wheel.
Crazy stuff! she said, grabbing it back
'Ow's the best way to write, make some money,
without me appearin' a bleedin' fool?'
I bought her vodka, suggested a sitcom.
Blackly funny Dostoevsky, gulped down in a shot.
'I'll help you write it' I lied. 'See you next week.'
She flinched as I gambled not even a cent.
'Ave to consult with me ball and chain…
out most early evenings, bar Thursday night.'
Thursday arrived, she didn't turn up.
About to leave. A restaurateur laughed.
Told a tale of a casino and cheering food.
A literate woman, conspiring in the kitchen,
arranged caviar and truffles on Salome's plate.
Then smugly observed an unconsoled gambler
dispense gloom, of his loss, by rarefied eating.
Was that my writer preparing material?
Juicy tit bits arranged for late night TV?
Or was she now sinking, with her ball and chain,
into debt, money schemes and mad risks
some unproduced, defiantly headless, wonder?

Possum at the Palace

"We had this rather lugubrious man in a suit, and he read a poem…I think it was called 'The Desert.' And first the girls got the giggles, and then I did and then even the King. 'The Desert, Ma'm?' Wilson asked. 'Are you sure it wasn't called The Waste Land? 'That's it. I'm afraid we all giggled. Such a gloomy man, looked as though he worked in a bank, and we didn't understand a word."

Queen Mother in conversation with A.N.Wilson.

"I'm a bit of a ruin that Cromwell knocked about a bit."

Marie Lloyd

These fragments I have shored against my ruins.

T.S.Eliot

Broken of sandal, Eliot stumbled through the desert.
Dying for a glass of water, home, bed, the cuddle of a cat.
Poor Tom couldn't believe the guffaws, the giggles,
the coughs, the snorts and the sniggers.
The king coughed to keep his king face straight.
All the princesses shook. One regally wet herself.
Jerusalem, Athens, Alexandria, Vienna, Mayfair,
Cheapside…and even the palace walls, were rising,
from their ruins, to mock him away.
Announcing the thunder, a corgi snapped at his feet.
Lacking air and sympathy, Stearns almost fainted.
This wasn't how I should have come across.
Not at all, not at all, not at all!

Eliot desired some bowler hatted cool. Pound roared
in his head. *Keep to yer vision when reading to monarchs!*
He'd expected too much from The Family.
Hoping their dignity and repose would make
humble inroads into Tom's high modernism.
Faint applause. Tepid champagne. Silence.
A flummoxed T.S.E. was ushered away.

(the footman smiled. *Queer cut for The Palace*).
At Victoria tube, the middle classes were very quiet.
Tired Tom ached for cries of working class delight.
Like when Marie Lloyd had sparred with an audience.
She'd sung, from her lusty stage, of their old man.
Fine, but Eliot couldn't dilly dally his introspection.

If only the people would love Eliot's mind.
Let the verse, fragmented fresh peas, in a decaying pod,
get deep down inside yer. Good Waste Land eats.
Mashed with potato. Washed down with a pint.
Quotes, allusions, and funny foreign words.
Greedily eaten by all aspiring to be raised up.

Let no one walk behind, in front or beside you, Tom.
Let's have Possum eating canned peaches and caring
for old Prufrock, now wearing fashionable shorts.
Madly & happily bald. Never again caught drowning
in a sea of royals. Just wowing all the excitable mermaids!

Decadence

Cracks in the bedroom wall now, spreading each day.
Air bubbles trapped by truth, paint and wallpaper.
Hand bursting through. A crying out to make sense,
be remembered. The sharing of a prophecy.

One day the wall will laugh at such effort.
Crumble and vanish. Over the hammer a mournful chant.
Broken concrete. Scattered dust. Vast new swamp
covering a city, in flux, that tried to stand up.
We might still need our bedroom in the mud.
Disturbing old bones, aching to sleep.

Perhaps it was Plato's hand bleeding against the concrete
and plaster; grasping for a noble lie to seal the damage.
He thought all poetry was a decadent lying.
Then is this poem only some falling away
into the earth, with nothing left to hit against,
speak up for, shed a tear or decline?

Meeting with a Terrorist

I thought we'd meet on a plane.
Or on a crowded bus or train.
I realised a hired car was out,
too small and intimate.
As for getting together on a bicycle,
you laughed at the idea.

Always in the moment though.
Opening yourself up to me
and someone later who'd
promised you a meeting.

To feel the full passionate blast
there has to be a blasted off face.
You know where you are then.
Where you stand, or don't.

But the other thing was different.
I didn't expect you to bring that.
I ran towards your covering,
spreading southwards. Invisible.
In the north it was clean. But boring.
First symptoms. First impressions.
If I re-run will you do it again?

I embrace my nightmare's lover.
Radiate me. Right up to the end.
Fear & desire. You gave me so much

La Strada Finisce

I ate pistachios from an ashen grey tree
in Bronte at the base of Mount Etna.
Sharpened volcanic pellets hanging wild
and warm on their knotted branches.
Full of seedy unripeness,
making biscuits or ice cream
perfectly dammed.
I threw them onto the narrowing road.
Picked up my camera,
adjusted its hungering lens.

A woman dressed in forlorn blue
with her old, gnarled, half naked father
were seated (like lovers) on a broken bench.
La strada finisce! she cried, hand plucking.*
She offered pistachios, born of her property,
then withdrew, arm in arm, with the old nakedness.

Obediently I tasted her offering.
Compensation, or simply poison,
for daring to photograph a distant friend
and neighbour, that higher up
indifferent lava?

La strada finisce = literally, the end of the road

Tourist Visiting the Anus of the World

There's an excellent restaurant in Auschwitz town.
The bigos is delicious. The beer's so cool.
Soup thickened with vegetable.
Pancake swimming in jam.

One hour before the last train back,
a man ravenously ate his dinner.
Trying to forget a stodgy lunch,
the camp museum's café potato,
gravy and meatball buried
on a cracked white plate.

On the platform he read of a Polish gardener
who stole extra supplies, for the ever hungry
commandant's wife.
Frau Hesse cooked good meals at home,
her 'paradise', with children and flower beds,
three miles away from the wire.

The SS commandeered the last restaurant.
Squatting on stools carved out by labourers.
Devouring haunches of roast hare,
washed down with schnapps,
on the long table.

'Anus of the world' wrote Dr.Kremer
in his diary, then hastily blotted the ink;
smudging a beautiful
calligraphy before a kiss
and the taking of supper.

Garuda Bird Mask Cracking

In the village of Peliaton he dreamt of Garuda and Mozart.
Eagle pecking at his ear. Ramayana's dance. Mozart's requiem mass.
White wine, fried noodles and pineapple proved to be the upstart.
Belly ache over festival fire. Balinese dream came out of his ass.

Music swelled in his aching brain. Perfumed with rose damask.
Fluttering martially at the door. Garuda bird of the nation state.
Wolfgang Amadeus opened up. Here stood a stranger with a task.
Message & money dropped in M's lap. The commission's very late.

Bird death - head approached. Mozart pressed a cloth to a face.
He woke up screaming. *Rex tremendae* accompanying the crack of glass.
A foot was pushed through a naked window (at home there was lace).
No curtain to shield you. Too far away, to bolt into the past.

Morning brought evidence of dreams, sweat and imagination.
Broken window paid for. Foot back from nightmare, unharmed.
Now, the burying of images. East kicking west for the exhumation.
His partner hides Garuda in her backpack. They won't be alarmed.

The Traveller
(For A)

A thousand and one hotel rooms.
Some with fans, a hard bed, or minus a lock,
carefully balanced by air conditioned views.
A hotel in Calcutta. You dressed in cotton batik,
posed crazy with a battered 'Lonely Planet.'

A cow on the road blocking the traffic.
Calmly you sat beside the beast.
Your stomach blown up, a cancerous balloon.
It's coming. It's spreading. It's mine alone!
You clung to the earth. The cow got up.

I woke from my dream, groping for the real Calcutta.
That long night of refusing hostels.
We'd camped with a crowd at the railway station.
I'd slept for a moment. Then you were gone.
Searching the streets. Fearing abduction.

Running back towards the dirty waiting room.
I found you, tenderly surprised at my panic.
We tightly embraced. Love was now breathing.
Gently sitting down. Children ready for collection.
A mother, eating rice, placed our hands in her meal.

Ten years later alone in Sicily. I wandered the coast.
My guidebook stuffed with her printed e mails.
Tales of doctors who opened and probed.
Their suitcases filled with instruments of tourism.
Your body caught, booked, mapped out in advance.

A husband had now invaded all your rooms.
To finally guard the door of the hospice.
Three times I asked to visit. Three times denied.
She dying must respond better. I reasoned distraught.
The family backpack was hooked to your shoulders.

We collected countries as if rare books.
Cheaply acquiring first editions,
India, Thailand, China, Laos, Vietnam.
Backpacked through exotica
and scribbled mad irreverent notes.

Assorted Histories

Man on a Mobile by Kindertransport Statue

Five children of copper coloured stone,
moulded in exile, with all the flight
of anxiety sculptured out of their faces.
Representatives for those who crossed Germany,
to the Hook of Holland, and sailed to the ports
of Harwich and Southampton,
where London Quakers applauded,
housed and silently bed the last Jews down.

Like a cat the businessman claws mobile from ear.
Free to scan his caught day of dazzling web pages.
His copper patterned, zipped up, leisure bag
confidently wedged on the children's plinth.

These statues' suitcases are older and heavier affairs.
Unlike thirties leather they bear no plastered hotel
stickers of exotic locations, with captive sunspots.
Celebrity toffs once flashed that kind of bulk
luggage in a decade of hate and Semitic stars.
Today, stone children with number tags.
Designer label on flexible bag.

What if they chose other times and destinations?
That the man travelled back to Buchenwald, in 1940,
minus his pages and business plan.
Whilst the group's little girl, holding her teddy bear,
and waving at him, was turned into skin and bone,
for a daytrip to Southampton in 2011.

Yet the mischief of history is crueller, less fanciful;
planting itself in the rough here and now.
Transportation for a statue, inside its crate,
or businessman, in his car,
is a short journey, computerised
through a careful peace.

Festive End

Boy, in a sailor suit, posing. Acutely confident. Pristine.
Hand placed on British Cavalry Horse. Superior carving.
Father's afternoon servants. Shaped into willing toys.
Shopping catalogue model. Infant Edwardian thingness.
Push handle, detachable harness, wooden base and removable wheels.
Will be the pride of any boy or girl lucky enough to own one.
Sweating horses, under the thing's grip, riding a toyland empire,
butchered in the early pouring fields of France and Belgium.
First carnage autumn over. Dead nag swapped, for caterpillar tank.

Sales of lead soldiers. Gamage's store outdid their rivals' glut.
Cheaper, ungassed, unbroken, unfinished, trench friendly.
Out of battle, come the customers. Unleaded of spirit.
Eager to confront armies in the basement grotto.
Little Holborn boy, now yearning. To be dressed
as a young man forever? Smearing mud on his khaki chest.
Shop assistant cleans hands, cries.
Now, jump up child onto the counter. Trot well your father's glory.
Photographer hiding under a cloth. A nightmare photographs well.
Father on leave. Sullen captain. Lost in an anxious cavalry mind.
Outraged by his kin, defacing memory of older battle dreams.
Burnt by an arsonist grief. Choking to speak to the new manager.

Gamage's Christmas Bazaar, nineteen thirteen.
Lying on a library table in twenty ten.
Nineteen seventy two reprint of all the ephemera
we once needed, or thought we needed,
for the festive end.

Invasion of Mars

They observed a boy named Philip Mars.
Superior to any watery organism
you might discover on the red planet.
Yet spoilt. Conceited. Up for bullying.

Vandals pushed him to the ground.
Probed him with an eager penknife.
Blood dripping onto a record player.
Expensive. With cutting edge speakers.

Philips' stronger half never rose up
as the bossy son of a Roman god
sound tracked by Holst. Stupid boy.
With stupid music. Of stupid parents.

Minds sharpened like prowling Martians.
Counting money, they sat and waited.
Trapped in his fragile earthling home,
timid & bandaged, a watching Mars.

Certain Shops

Junk shop, newsagent, hardware store, grocers,
emporium, bazaar, even telephone booth.
A multi limbed shop. Its owner fidgety for business.
Drumming his fingers on a battered counter.
Here Father slyly stole bundles of firewood,
whilst paying, up front, for Condor tobacco.
Ashamed, Mother covered her face with 'Woman's Realm'.
Clutching my comic book, I called on
Desperate Dan, as if a Viking God,
to burn the wood and forgive us.

When domiciled in Camden, I once got drunk
and harangued the police – to deal with the other police
who stormed a battle zone in Toxteth.
Reviled the newspaper for its photograph.
My unclassifiable shop now burnt down.
Rioters may have just causes
for murdering a special place.

London shop fronts with ageing curtains, fading posters,
broken windows and the corrosive smell of bleach.
Old un-curiosity shops, that Dickens would have loathed.
Certain shops should mindfully die, when we are young.

Unnamable Journey

I never imagined Samuel Beckett in a nursing home.
Beckett's sojourn was at Le Tiers Temps (The Third Age).
My mother stayed at Sun View Residence.
She wrote shopping lists for Father, five years dead,
then slowly tore them up.
In a spidery hand Sam wrote
his last poem, watched rugby on television
and carefully avoided the dining room.

Mother at twenty. Spying a singer,
on stage, that she wished to imitate.
Beckett recalling a childhood hymn.
Handing it over to Krapp
for his tape recorder.

Now the day is over / night is drawing nigh.
Shadows of the evening / Steal across the sky.

I can't translate their unnameable journey.
Yet through singing, in the final months,
their lungs breathed in such evidence
of trial, part escape, maybe blessing.

Mother sang to me over breakfast,
before nine on a Liverpool Boxing Day.
Beckett was buried, at eight thirty, in Paris.
No hymn. No priest. No speeches made.
A cold day, at Montparnasse, claimed
for the feast of St.Stephen alone.

Troy Merchandise

At Troy stands a seventies wooden horse.
A knocked out adventure playground thing.
Fondled by reverent Japanese tourists.
Stiff. Infantile. An unhorsey embarrassment.
Whilst at Cannakale lies a Hollywood horse.
A spectacular prop donated for the city image.
Giant rough animal on guard by the river.
Noble. Assured. Wooden of ego. Wisely marketed
as wily ancient. Celebrity greater than a movie star.

The horse isn't armed with trappings of gold.
Yet contains more doors for invading warriors.
Fashioned with all the right on recyclables.
Discarded wood, from the hull of a wrecked ship,
proudly displaying its nautical scales.
Environmental wear and tear held together
by fisherman ropes. Looking dragged from the sea.
Tenderly dried for its weeping soldiers.

A tourist ploughed the market for a souvenir,
some glossy mark of Troy, to fit in a suitcase.
(That ancient wound. Cutting deeper than the arrows
of today's media, as Homer wretches copious over
bad Homer films.) Yet Hollywood's franchise failed.
No spin off horse to stroke, all the way home.

Two am. Unable to sleep. Needing cigarettes and air.
Tourist now dressed. Walked to the riverside.
Smoked and considered a world without wars.
Impossible. The Trojan guys were constantly at it.
Indefinitely prolonging a futile battle. Dragging out
the heroics. (Now, we tie things up with ropes
of diplomacy. Then sabotage, cunning and fast.
Dupe with our 'smarter' horses. Open the trap doors.
Drop missiles at night. Calibrate the killing.)

His thoughts, souring with the curling smoke,
were broken by a woman, with a ladder.
She climbed up. Placed a hand on the horse's flank.
Spoke Greek of a kind he couldn't fathom.
Her tone was seductive, imploring, insistent.
Stepping out from the kiosk, he heard the names
she called - Menelaus, Leonteus, Odysseus.

Drunk she descended. Ran off down the street.
He climbed the ladder. Tapped thrice on the horse.
Said 'Helen has gone' and crazily waited.
Only the wind, blowing hard and strong, replied
that Winter was coming from the north.

Helen wasn't imprisoned forever to Paris's bed.
She returned to Menelaus. Homer evolved a cosy couple.
Daughter Hermione was constantly told the big adventure.
One day, maybe bored, she sat whittling a toy horse,
desiring admiration beyond her Spartan home.
Troy merchandise.
True deliverance.
True conquest.

Cats of Venice

Proud trances of cats
traverse piazzas.
Lagooned to blend
with architecture.
Their skinny fur bones
of arrogant mystery
were carnival spawned
to purr at history.

The Other Boy

Wounded by adult keepers.
Blasted by street children.
A boy ran for sanctuary in the park.

He was tense, afraid to remove his shirt.
Allow the sun's rays to stake out his chest.
Pawing at his neck, the heat tried to break him.
Eyes squinted at the sun's fiery unclothed disc
then shut quick as the first button was undone.

Discarding of shirt. Rapid beat of heart.
Ribs palmed by the sun. Stroked into foreplay.
He wanted to be taken, but wasn't that day.
Radiantly alone in a sensual underpinning;
offering up his arms to the sky.

Forty seven years later he found it again.
That patch of grass verdantly close to the cricket ground.
Now in the old creased space, under a new fiercer sun,
a man savagely fell asleep.

A teenager woke him and asked for the time.
He couldn't speak of the hour, what it meant now.
Badly sunburnt the other boy edged away.

Colour my movie, Miss Niah from Mars

'Settings, dialogue, characterisation and special effects are of a low order; but even their modest unreality has its charm. There is really no fault in this film that one would like to see eliminated. Everything, in its way, is quite perfect.'
    Monthly Film Bulletin review of *Devil Girl from Mars* (1954)

Perception 1

We offered haggis. A bed for the night. A Scottish inn.
Yet earthling sex slaves were top of your list.
Men to breed women on the barren red planet.
Was that really my Devil Girl, so starkly
black and white, on dvd?
Oh colourise my celluloid dream.
Change wardrobe, please.
Smear brown your lips. Pink flesh your face.
Shine bright in emerald s & m gear
your skirt, cowl, cap and stiletto boots.
Let the Hoover shaped robot helper
be high tech gold out of control
and your promiscuous ray gun
spurt a laser beam
all feisty red
and cobalt blue.

Perception 2

B picture heather turns purple green.
Bewildered Scotsman evaporates on the glen.
Whilst his rounded up NHS glasses,
and smoking remains, reek of pale skin.

Perception 3

Five years old.
My paint box was very small.
Miss Niah commanded.

Monochrome
(in praise of black & white cinema)

Above all the detail so faithful in its lover's way.
Saturating reality, whether in studio or on location.
Making you ache to be inside its grainy texture.
Film then desired a supreme density.
Dark celluloid pigmentation.
Black and white amassing.
Willing all shades of grey.

Such beautiful hue of monochrome body.
Where a cameraman, through a passionate lens,
crafted the producer's dream.
Of the silents, critics wrote of silver toned prints.
Projected on screens as large as cathedral towers.
And when film spoke, photographers found other tools
to subdue the voices, continue its evolving lustre.

We were made to look askance at nature's flowers,
plants, trees and other Technicolor excuses.
For this was the first great home of cinema.
Its limited spectrum replacing how we'd
once boundlessly viewed all nature.
To be blinded of all other colours,
and yet not bothered.

Such uncluttering of the retina
to calmly shape a tense design
and crazily pursue a director's look.

Silly beautifying things
like the flirting angle
of a camera feisty
for an actor's cheekbones.

Each madly ambiguous image.
Each seductive darkness.
Each vision of light.

Hopeless Romantic

Young woman. Petite. Brunette.
Wearing very short denim shorts.
Two words in a style of Victorian gothic.
Hopeless Romantic. Tattooed on her thighs.
I, and my bored friend, have sat through
a Hungarian film school western placed
experimentally in the American Civil War.
Cheeky tattoo letters are dancing
on the whiteness of her train shook flesh.
A perfect deflection from the aesthetic
problems of avant garde cinema.

As she stands up, we more fully appreciate
the charm of the girl's self-advertisement.
Both sighing now. A wry appreciation
of the hopelessness of all romantics.
Exiting the train, she smiles
and blows us the most natural of kisses.
Johnny comes marching home again.
Hurrah! Hurrah!

League of Nations

She obtained a Nazi flag and took it to a pub and let people pay 6d
a time to spit on it. She finally sold it for 10 shillings having made
a total of £2.10 shillings 0d.

(The actions of a maid from the Woodstock Hotel in Islington, 1945)

I shall dye it black. Wear a V.E. headscarf.
No. It will give me horrible lice.
I shall bathe away the war. It will be my towel.
No. It will poison the pores of my skin.
I shall drape it over my bed.
No. Party fleas are still in abundance.
I shall cover the cracks in the dining room table.
No. More worms will crawl out of the wood.
I shall fashion it into a noose.
No. I have not been promised a neck.
Oh God, I shall throw it onto a bonfire.
No. It can turn itself into a snake, a book, a promise.
Oh what shall I do with their flag?
Oh what shall I do with their flag?
They are defeated.
I must rejoice.
I must.

Ninety six people spat on its colours
before & after their lukewarm beer.
Ninety six liberated Londoners. Jubilant
with jubilant coins of the realm.
When the ninety seventh purchased
the flag of phlegm, its cloth spoke up.

Make more money, my friend.
Keep me for V.J. Day. To partner
my Japanese Red Sun.
Further victory brings more thirst.
More drinks. More clearing of throats.
More empires to unfurl.

Outfoxing Hyenas

'They say that hyenas change their nature every year, so that sometimes they are male and sometimes female. So when a hyena saw a fox and criticized her for having spurned her friendly overtures, the fox replied, 'Don't blame me! Blame your own nature, which makes it impossible for me to tell whether you would be my girlfriend or my boyfriend!'

Aesop's Fables, translated by Laura Gibbs

'I want to stay Adolf, not become Anna.'
Mistakenly Hitler ate the meat of a sly hyena.
The black fox limped. His body ambiguous.
Bewildered by deep forests. Which way to turn?
'My Fuhrer I've turned you into a cabaret diva.'

A feisty propaganda show captured by Goebbels.
War plans altered. Audience stormtrooped.
Adolf languidly smoking a foreign cigarette.
Doomed to change gender, without his asking.
Nazi sexual organs. Nastily transformed.

'Our real hyena, with sexy legs, did a bunk.'
Sure, Goebbels, sure. Dietrich cleared off
to radiantly vamp. USA branded her shapely calves.
Beautifully lit veils - a studio of fish nets.
Hollywood's jungle eclipsed the Black Forest.

'The Queen of UFA can have all she wants…
our Fuhrer would like you to come back home.'
Goebbels desired Dietrich to lick all Germany.
Marlene faced his emissary. 'Never…never!'
(F.B.I. files recorded each step to her never.)

She could have returned, sat next to Adolf / Anna.
Removed his wholesome Eva - kicked out the Braun.
Plunged her jewelled dagger into his pulsating neck.
Tossed away the cyanide pill. Flown back to L.A.
But propagandists own the dreams of foxes and hyenas.

That German fabulist would have filched the knife
from Dietrich's garter – no bunking off now.
Leaving Hitler biting Marlene's other irresistible thigh.
More hyenas of womanhood, invading Adolf's being.
Whilst Dietrich's overtaken by his girly advances.

Adolf, tied to Anna, was escorted to prison.
Goebbels put in charge of production – chasing hyenas.
Enemy unchanged. The war dragged on. No end in sight.
Minus movie stars, assassinations or 'what if' history.
No obvious outcomes for foxy fables.

Destinies

Sumimasen, Sumimasen

Rule secured London. So easily smashed.
Emergency alarm pulled. Passing mood.

To be caught anxious. Japanese, alone.
Inhibition, her crime. Delaying full train.

I said three minutes to departure.
Did you not hear me, woman?

Stop train again - all customers leave!
She watched herself. Wrecking the crowd.

Coil of humiliation. Driver sprung tight.
Down she fell. Into the mechanism.

Her small frame shook, so violent.
A sobbing. A calling. Entering shame.

Blistering tears flowed down her cheeks.
Seeking early water. Flood of etiquette.

Family lake where rules float holy.
You must not shudder the surface.

This shaken place of others' authority.
Conduct strewn outside its broken gate.

Driver broods. Her parents invade city.
Clashing duties. Will you sleep tonight?

Sumimasen, sumimasen.*

* Japanese for sorry

Sleeping Sickness
(a cut up poem for Patricia Maguire)

The creature in all the world most to be envied is Patricia Maguire of Chicago. She sleeps since 1931, her stupor lightens briefly at meal times. She is massaged daily, her fan mail is composed mostly of proposals of marriage.
(letter from Samuel Beckett to Mary Manning Howe 18/1/1937)

She sleeps, mostly composed of her Chicago.
The envied fan mail of daily marriage.

1931 massaged proposals
in the world of creature Patricia.

since briefly, at meal times, all her stupor lightens
the most she is
is to be Maguire

in all the world since 1931 is The creature
of daily marriage.

Maguire sleeps, at meal times, composed
of her fan mail of Chicago.
mostly envied, her stupor lightens

to be massaged most
briefly of Patricia
she is
She is

Patricia sleeps 1931
Maguire daily in her since world.

she is her proposals of the massaged fan mail
is her creature, composed at meal times

marriage stupor mostly lightens
She, of all Chicago,
is to be envied
The most.

Total Melancholia, Winter 1976

So freezing a hostel kitchen. Radiators on high.
As high as the windows on black condensation.
My stew burned on the stove. I turned off the gas.
Through the cooking steam, came a high grinning man
hurtling himself at my cold table.

Don't murder the vegetables. They're holy.
When I was young, I sailed to an island
where vegetables died, or vanished along
with the fruit, fish and birds.
They called it Christmas Island.
It even gave me a Christmas present.
Navy discharge on psychiatric grounds.
My total melancholia.

He revealed a battered book from a stained bag
with Buddhist designs. Mantras read over my meal.
Dessert was marihuana, wine, more Bhagavad-Gita.
As I crashed, he cried out like a Job, covered
in the sores, of the navy's incompetence.

When the flash came, it was fluorescent. I saw my
hand, man…an incredible x-ray…right to the bone.
I felt such a heat, as if in an oven. My body was like
hellfire. We didn't look back. Heard explosions in
the air. Then thrown to the ground. When we turned
round, a rainbow was cutting through a mushroom
cloud. We were guinea pigs. Just trained to look, man,
only look!

In my drunken sleep, a megaphone voice came out
of the whirlwind – warning all stationed men
to stay silent and try to avoid
the falling coconuts.

Palawa

Tasmanian aboriginal people knew the kangaroo as a creation spirit and ancestor of Palawa the first man. Before transformation from Kangaroo to man, Palawa had no knee joints and could not sit down. The spirit Droemerderer broke his legs and cut of his tail, giving him a place to stay and live.

Greg Lehman, The Palawa Voice

Bereft of ancestral kneecaps.
Unable to sit down in their world.
Red dust on shoes leaving no mark.
Darker stains, of the shopping mall, cajoling
– glue, petrol and alcohol washing down
bread & chips as they sleepwalk wild.
Here's a dream landscape for nomads
clutching welfare cards and feisty children.

A parade of goods at Yeperene's centre.
This desert retreat, of shops and counters,
waterhole linked by an escalator down
to a grand piano, fountain accompaniment
and a crowd cannily intersecting
with a bright competition car.

A Palawa girl scuffs her jeaned bottom against its doors.
Mother, bright with substances, grips the bonnet.
Father laughs, removes cap, salutes an absent driver.
Loudspeakers fall quiet announcing the winner.
The crowd disperses. The family changes tack.
They push over grandmother, caught un-demented.
Scraggy body, in wheelchair, that can't drive the children.

Security man wakes up from colonial sleep.
Grandmother's taken to a grassier verge.
Old woman pulsating with kangaroo urges.
Lined pouch for her dreams. Ancient knees re-born
Cops and relatives policing sacred ground,
as she crawls, walks or jumps all the way home.

Beyond Yeperene and its rubbish bins
stretches a long orphaned outback.
No security now on a moveable earth.
Lost & illegal, the land wants to own you.
Earth's tormenting, reclaiming arms.

To Lift the Voices

Blind, he listens to a shellac disc of lieder.
Nuances the ear to catch inflections on the wing.

A pause. A breath. The pattern secreted before the note.
All that furthers music calmly engineered.

Restorer accompanies the daunting tread of singer,
doleful pianist and Schubert on their winter's day.

Cylinder, shellac, vinyl, tape. Containers of baritione.
Leaving each imperfect vessel. *Winterreise* pounds the ear.

Gloom of an organ grinder, trapped by technical blemish.
Unbroken Schubert seeds his progress of despair.

Enthusing each measured step. Joyful of our outcome.
With dark precision, an engineer cleans artefact.

Snowflakes, real and mind like, blow into his room.
White formatted. On his desk, freezing the headphones.

Another's winter intrudes on songs' journey.
He cannot picture, only feel the cold of heartbreak.

The window's shut. In solitude he rests assured.
Closing down the sounds that never fade within.

Pianist and singer stalk the shifting journey. Each shock
cleaning interpretation. Restorer drinks a warming wine.

Small each gesture for the anxious archive. Larger perhaps
his sense of consolation. Master, of the sonic, lifts the voices

Sonata

Three seagulls squawking.
Landing on roof slope.
Fog framing window.
Masking of light.
Melodia. Adagio.
Torchlight of violinist.
Grey afternoon.
Perfect phrasing.
Searching Bartok.

Layered lament.
Pitched to flight.
All is *pianissimo.*
Hushed fluttering.
Bird notes deepening.
Presto agitato.
Opening of window.
Flap vanishing wings.

Seagulls snapping
Bela from their sky.

Brought to time

'Me time' she cries. 'I need more quality me time'
Her friend opposite nods back out of fear.

Why should time be specially designated?
Quantified for her alone?
As if time, for the *me,* were being prepared.
Like her meal now in this busy restaurant.

She looks forty, same as the table number.
A waiter serving up time. Choice cuts
of animal fate. Rare. Medium. Well done.

In the rare time, you're given a reprieve.
Rapture for the few. Time is underdone.
More innocently cooked.

Tasting the medium. Unseasoned.
Banal of flavour. Time put up with.
Routine. No ritual dressing on the meat.

Served well done. Possibly smug.
Never quite burnt time. Self congratulating.
But was the food authentic?

Cutlery attacks. Me time, your time, our time.
Pleases. Deflects. Feeds illusions.
Satisfies, for a moment, our role.

Cracks on the surface of the golden bowl.
Nothing's labelled. Nothing's that certain.
She must learn to adapt.
Memory comes and goes.
All is a shedding.
brought to time.

Hat

(for A)

Susan inducing birthday
in French restaurant
wearing so blue a hat
who this belonging to now
when mind's eye blinking
yes i am knowing well
as Laura my dead
partner removing hat
from Susan placing
lopside on head then
journeying innocent table
worn by friend & stranger
guests handing round
a creased felt thing
pausing on tense scalps as
i picking up knife & fork
placing food into the hole
in my face to nourish
Laura's abandoned hat
resting headless by bread
removed adroitly by waiter
for coming of dessert to
Laura standing vacant eyes
mystery begging to be reading
menu ordering wine gazing
at guests whispering
through Susan's ear as i
hole with crying face
shutting out desire
to touch her side.

Whistling
(for M.R.James)

Found on a beach, hidden
in Templar masonry.
Not a whistle for
a broken teacher,
fraught referee
or nervous policeman.
Very old, but deceptively
modern in shape, as if
for excitable dogs
who would probably
die of fright,
if they heard it.
Waiting to call up
a Norfolk wind
that will back off,
frantically afraid
of its terrible sound

So blow and provoke
the ghastly ancient one
to run towards you,
locate your room,
turn the key in the door
and make chaos
of the spare tidy bed
that defends your reason.

The thing is always
a personage,
never a person,
with a face of crumpled linen.
Its slow shifting creases
would continue to horrify

ordinary hotel sheets
if they could be revived
to tell their tale
to a beaten pillow
thrown to the floor.

American Dramaturge
(for Tom)

You read Sophocles in a stumbling ancient Greek.
Revered Shakespeare. Were cool to Pirandello,
seduced by Tennessee, fixated by Beckett
and when teaching O'Neil you shone.
Capturing the fine things for writing drama
with its tricky need to resonate quick
every word and action on the hoof.

The offstage world grew dark.
Teaching stopped. You were dying.
Yet a fragment, of theatre, refused to grow ill.
You, that skinny kid in his twenties,
in the front of the stalls
for 'West Side Story'.
At its premiere you gawped at the gang fights,
almost swooned disbelieving the music, devoured
each satirical melodic swipe
then finally drank the pain
of its street unwise
Romeo and Juliet.
Somewhere was now the planet.
Buzzing to write (of the magic circle) you spilled out
with the crowd into a bigger, more exciting street.

That kind young man, made hip by Broadway,
rode forty years of seminars.
Breaking in his clever anxious students,
he caught the real writers (flung
between their Sharks and Jets)
sharpened the mind, tightened the craft,
averted a rumble, avoided the cops,
focused the play
to let it go free.

Death of a young Kabuki Prince

Gouging of a redundant soldier's eye.
Corpse of a baby shoved back in the womb.
Woman beaten to death with an oar.
Emperor's head decapitated for a trophy.
Kabuki killings are as common as breathing.
Shells of intrigue, jealousy and revenge

exploding naturally on the feudal plain.

Yet when a nine year old prince was sacrificed
a man sat up in the stalls, engaged by the war.
Such a tender graceful slipping away.
An eerie skilful talent for dying; praising
father, his kingdom and heaven's approach.

From the balcony, another man cried *Kakeye! Kakeye!*
This request for the name of the actor's father
is the highest praise you can bestow.
Tonight a son died well on a stage.
Even his stage family were pleased.
Are you not proud of him, all you fathers?
And which good father did he please most?

Literacy Lesson

The boy's a raw alphabet, ineffably strong.
His language is wonder so deeply hidden.
If a word struggles up, sworn or spat out,
fresh air it will lack in our sucked ABC.

Unknowing he hates the literacy of all
whose sounds have lost their primal margin.
With brutal defences tongues sadly get by
as we cough away an unsociable phlegm.

Without our words the boy has no power.
The teacher's a power because of the boy.
We give him puberty to the din of the world.
Falsetto to bass, the breaking voice falls.

Minotaur Salesman

(After Picasso's illustrations for The Vollard Suite)

A bullish salesman cornered the Pyrenees,
selling oriental rugs to the bourgeoisie.
One day, before shaving, the mirror cracked.
Another bull emerged. Horns ripping the carpet.

Desiring freedom from his family,
that unending maze of debit and credit,
a former chic resident of the city of Pau
became an unshaven minotaur.

Two boys, two girls and a severed wife
were his mental snacks inside the labyrinth.
Theseus came. Looked. Then left. We wrongly
imagined him yielding an axe to fell you.

Touching Ariadne up, in her fifteenth year.
You pulled her hard against your body.
Your daughter, with her gentle string,
vacillating over the right way out.

Innocence was cleaved on a sullen afternoon.
Sales targets – made hard, erect and profitable.
The old bull redeemed his catchment area.

After violation she'd no other choice
but to blind you. Lost girl, with a fluttering dove,
leading the bull with a white stick.

At night, through the border country, he stumbled.
Arrived at Biarritz harbour. Never to see the fishermen,
the sail of the ship or view the stars from the river.

Minotaur salesman blocked
from the voyage back
to carpet a waiting floor
or furnish a simpler home.

Read me a motorway, Darling

'Old copies of Mills & Boon romantic novels are being used to help prolong the life of the UK's newest road the M6 toll…the novels were pulped at a re-cycling firm in South Wales …the pulp acts as a sound barrier.'

BBC News Webpage 2003

Romances shacked up with motorways.
Forty thousand novels, laid at every mile,
Charity shops and libraries ache to be vacuumed
of the ended of shelf life & remaindered damaged.
Fantasies for illiterate students, the old,
the unemployed and, too often, the wilfully sad.
Each has their torrid fix. A book's thrown
down, to gush alone on the sofa,
whilst another waits for a pick up.
For all that sweaty sentimental vanity
still desires to probe and burrow.
Words, having screwed the value of words,
gang up in each others maudlin paperback.
Minus a readership stories are beaten back,
led helpless and screaming, as if to an abattoir.
But it's merely the consoling factory of pulp
silencing four pounds ninety nine voices.
Fictions plummet into a sandwich of granite.
Become a sound barrier with asphalt & tarmac.
Crushed melodramas made cushions for cars.

'Other books are down there too!'
announced the tarmac spokesman.
'The Trial, The Odyssey, Don Quixote, Arabian Nights.'
Are these journey tales, in cheapo classic bindings,
carrying their own dysfunctional characters?
Joseph K, Ulysses, Don & Pancho,
plus an army of Arabic authors.
All fated to be squashed passengers.

Pressed hard against 'Good Read' characters
– those many aching virgins, lecherous tycoons,
sly secretaries and love struck widows.

The good and the great then.
The bad and a chemistry text book or two.
All mulched, at sunset, to make a little quieter
the cars, trucks, coaches, caravans and motorcycles
speeding home those dream book devourers.

Hot Disturbance at Primrose Hill

Smell the hill. Undulating with sweat & sun oil.
Barking dog runs for my flesh. Loud enough
to wake the tanning summer dead, t-shirt the living.
I snarl, as if canine too, and kick dog back
towards its horrified, let's casually walk now, owner.
On cue a college baseballer storms in; pitching
Americana to drown the sound of a lark, not ascending.
Predictably this spot's reserved for sport and crows.
Can I hate games then or scorn Ted Hughes?
Behind a tree, ipod and radio are triggered.
Wine bottle opened, beer can pulled, slurp & belch.
I stand up and dress to be inflicted by roaring planes
(such a flight controlled summer).
Exchange feet on grass, never I've decided as purely green
as the paddy fields of Vietnam, for a melting tarmac path.

I was reading an August newspaper, before the scorch
and squall tipped me over. Tensely inserted, between the crazy
season stories, was my faked bronzed skin and a patterned sky.
Now forced to swing back – make louder war on my enemies.
At the street entrance I shout in retaliation.
My imaginary army is pounding.
Beethoven, thunder and galloping horses.

Votive Offering

To be young. In a take away dwelling.
Night and day. Rhodes old town.
A kid, of a Greek. Slicing flakes
of lamb off a skewered carcass.
Watery eyes narrowed. Margin of meat.
Another souvlaki pushed as tight, as a cry,
into its paper cone, housed by fragments of salad.
Some chips as well says a voice.
Perturbed he throws away the late afternoon
dead chips. Cuts open a freezer bag and drops
fresh carbohydrate into a pan
of sizziling oil, coating everything.
Will you holiday at the end of the season?
Amazed he half looks at the voice's face,
snaps out, maybe two days rest, then Spain
and a job like this again.
Back faces customer. Chips frenziedly salted.
No. No. Just vinegar. He drops them, insanely hot,
drowned in malt, into their waiting cone.
They burn the hand, of the body, of the voice,
of the face he keeps lowering his eyes too.
Just a kid. Always working in high season.

Remission

cranberries pushed into honeyed porridge
blackening banana and milk captured
by steroid tabs over water dissolving
to stain bone marrow losing iron

charm of anti-oxidants
cajoling his frail body

recalling the food brought out in Keats
that Eve of St.Agnes lover
laying it on for his girl
spiced dainties
silken Samarcand
to cedar'd Lebanon

glowing hand on x-ray
tumour adoring the lung

no mana no dates no love food
argosy transferred from its route

Humanist Ceremony

Break any idea
of completed vision.
Just a delicate scan
of her boxed body,
maybe spirit, and hope
for a tender burning.

Sweat of handshakes.
A flush of stunned faces.
Ceremony over, they part.
Pressed into separate rooms.

Father. Husband. First lover.
On a cooler morning,
an unlocked door
will release the lover
she urgently needs.

For now it's an eruption
of uncovered cars,
mercilessly trapped
in August heat.
Stinging handles,
wheels and seats
burning
at the idea
of travelling home.

Calculation

"When do things end?" asked the child.
"They end when you die" replied the mother.
"Will I die soon...maybe next week?"
"No. You will live a long life...over seventy years."

The child counted, to himself, what was left of the mother.
After a minute, he grew tired.
"Can't add you up...it's hard!"
The mother laughed. "Don't place a number on me.
Think of an imaginary end...something endless...
nothing to add to...or subtract from...only a place
that's always been here...infinity."

She stood over the bed. Placed her hand on his brow.
Coming out of a fever, he said "Finity" After a pause came
...finity one...finity two...finity three...finity four...finity five....

Discarding Imagination

As a baby we gave birth to a baby.
Our searching hands reached out to touch
a hovering star made flesh & bone.
Doctor, nurse and midwife will not deliver
such children they cannot see or hear.

Babies, beyond the birth technicians,
breaking through their own backdoor.
Over gifted with life potential.
Duplicate, double or doppelganger
whispering wild ambitious plans.

Children, imagining a deeper genesis.
Serene but burning for a great container.
Adults attack their first light of mind.
Why always this wind shaking the leaves,
abandoning spring as we fell the trees?

Memory & Evidence

My front tooth has changed.
No longer a chipped remnant
gently nudging the unmarked
tooth next door. When probed by
my tongue, it had a roughness,
an edge. Felt strangely purposeful.

Filed down. Smoothed. Straightened.
Causing its neighbour to be shortened.
Tooth aligned with tooth.
Both trying to conform.
Join in a little better and faster
with the collective chewing.

I'd relished this dental 'imperfection'
as a sign of being human. A state of
tooth existed, without ever being
mad or wrong. Like the impossibility
of discovering perfect symmetry
in the human face.

Once, a child stole an orange off me.
I ran after him, down a back street.
I fell and my face hit the ground.
One hilly bruise and a broken tooth.
That dropped bitten orange and dirtied skin,
have disappeared, like the boy thief, forever.

I kept the look of a man with a broken
tooth badge. Indifferent to cosmetic change.
Untouched by vanity. Unselfconscious.
Then, fifty years later, compelled
by an obscure whim, I said
to the dentist, 'Correct it, please.'

I suppose I was weak. Capitulated.
Yet as my tongue now licks the repair,
I've nothing left to avenge
or forgive now. Time chases me,
and my blood red fruit,
along a different street.

Indigo Dreams Publishing
132, Hinckley Road
Stoney Stanton
Leicestershire
LE9 4LN
www.indigodreams.co.uk